Fruit Trees
of the Caribbean

Fruit Trees
of the Caribbean

Sandra Hewitt

MACMILLAN
CARIBBEAN

Macmillan Education
Between Towns Road, Oxford OX4 3PP
A division of Macmillan Publishers Limited
Companies and representatives throughout the world

www.macmillan-caribbean.com

ISBN: 978 1 4050 1845 6

Text © Sandra Hewitt 2005
Design and illustration © Macmillan Publishers Limited 2005

First published 2005

Designed and typeset by Carol Hulme
Illustrated by Tech Type
Cover design by Gary Fielder at AC Design
Cover photographs by Sandra Hewitt

The authors and publishers would like to thank the following for permission to
reproduce their photographs:

Sean Carrington p100; **William Cutts** pp 43, 52a, 52b, 78, 79, 80, 99, 106,
107; **Sandra Hewitt** pp 11, 12, 13, 14a, 14b, 15, 16, 17, 18a, 18b, 19, 20, 21,
22, 23, 24, 25, 26, 27, 28, 29, 30, 31, 32, 33, 37, 38, 39, 40, 41, 42, 44, 47,
48, 50, 51, 53, 54, 55, 56, 57, 58, 59, 60, 61, 62, 63, 64, 65, 66, 67, 68, 69,
71, 72, 74, 75, 76, 77, 81, 82, 83, 84, 85, 86, 87, 88, 89, 90, 91, 92, 93, 94,
95, 96, 97, 98, 101, 102, 103, 104, 105, 108, 109, 110, 111, 113, 114, 115,
116, 117, 118, 119, 120, 121, 122, 123, 124, 125, 126, 127, 128, 129, 130,
131, 132, 133, 134, 135, 136, 137, 138, 139, 140, front and back cover;
Alick Jones pp 1,2,6,8; **Natural Visions**/Heather Angel p45; **Science Photo
Library**/J.B. Rapskins p46; **Monica Warner** pp 34, 35, 36.

Printed and bound in Malaysia

2015 2014 2013 2012 2011 2010 2009 2008 2007
10 9 8 7 6 5 4 3 2

Contents

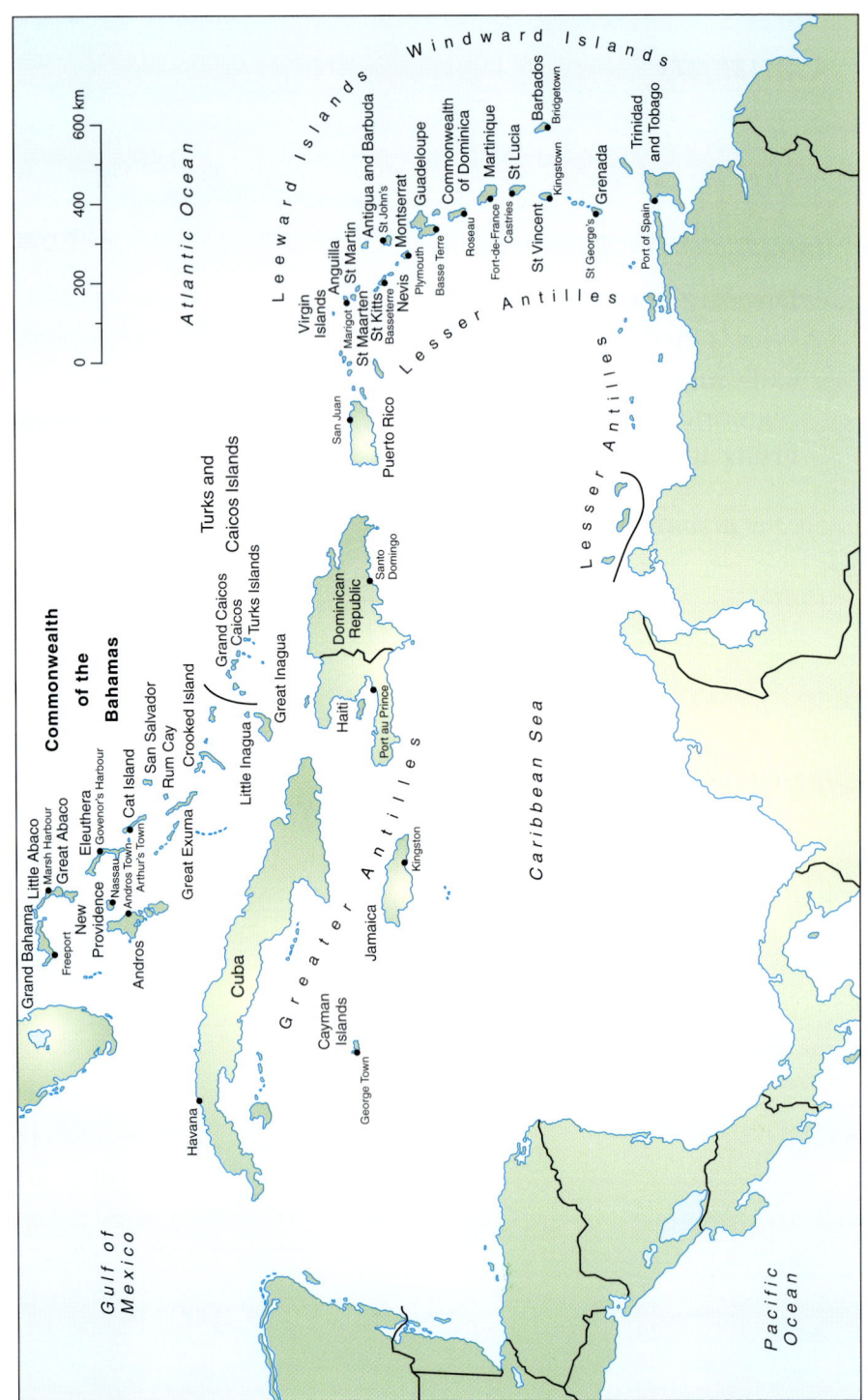

Windward Islands

Leeward Islands

Lesser Antilles

Atlantic Ocean

600 km

400

200

0

Barbados
Bridgetown

Trinidad and Tobago

Kingstown
St Vincent

Grenada
St George's

St Lucia
Castries

Martinique
Fort-de-France

Commonwealth of Dominica
Roseau

Guadeloupe
Basse Terre

Antigua and Barbuda
St John's

Montserrat
Plymouth

Nevis
Charlestown

St Kitts
Basseterre

St Maarten

St Martin
Marigot

Anguilla

Virgin Islands

San Juan
Puerto Rico

Port of Spain

Lesser Antilles

Turks and Caicos Islands

Grand Caicos
Caicos
Turks Islands

Great Inagua

Little Inagua

Crooked Island

Rum Cay

San Salvador

Cat Island

Eleuthera
Govenor's Harbour

Marsh Harbour
Little Abaco
Great Abaco

Grand Bahama
Freeport

Commonwealth
of the
Bahamas

New Providence
Nassau

Andros Town
Arthur's Town

Andros

Great Exuma

Santo Domingo

Dominican Republic

Haiti
Port au Prince

Cuba

Greater Antilles

Jamaica
Kingston

Cayman Islands
George Town

Havana

Caribbean Sea

Gulf of Mexico

Pacific Ocean

Introduction by Alick Jones

The imagery and symbolism of fruit conjure up such variety – visions of fertility and fecundity, of love and sin, creation and beauty, a sense of completeness and fulfilment. Little wonder that artists and poets have used this vocabulary for thousands of years and not surprising either, that we all respond to fruits in a more visceral way than their simple nutritional value deserves. From Eve's apple to the banana in Lynford Christie's lunch box we see more than simply something good to eat. The Caribbean region's huge range of fruit is thus one of the many attractive features that help to produce the sense of richness for residents and an exotic, yet tempting, novelty for visitors.

Tropical regions of the world are different from temperate ones in many aspects of fruit growing. In temperate areas most fruits are both strictly seasonal and mostly ripening from mid-summer through to late autumn ('season of mists and mellow fruitfulness'). Of course, modern storage and transportation methods give rich countries apples and strawberries all year round, but the association of fruit with summer is a deep-seated one for residents of both northern and southern latitudes. In the tropics there is 'seasonality' with some fruits but there is no 'off-season': always there is

The cooler climate of Jamaica's Blue Mountains produces some of the world's premier coffee

something coming in (or going out). 'Summer' as such hardly exists and wet and dry seasons are of rather more importance in the fruit calendar than temperature and day length. With other tropical fruits there is yet another benefit, namely that of year-round production. Furthermore, the inventory of available fruits in the Caribbean has been widened by the introduction of species from other parts of the tropical world such as Africa and Asia, as well as from nearby Central America. Some of these introductions, such as that of the breadfruit, have fascinating stories behind them. Others came in anonymously with the many waves of human immigration into the West Indian islands – Amerindians from South America, the Spanish and other Europeans, Africans, Indians, Chinese and so on.

In this book Sandra Hewitt has described more than 90 trees and their fruits. A few of them, whilst botanically known as fruits, will be known to many as spices, and at least one has been included because it must <u>not</u> be eaten. (This is the Manchineel, page 45, which produces fruit looking like small green apples but that are decidedly poisonous.) They range from the very familiar oranges and bananas through some that are appearing in

If rain threatens the trays can be pushed under the sheds for shelter

supermarkets in cooler parts of the world, such as mangoes and the paw-paw, to a number that are virtually unknown outside the region. Many of the fruits described do not fit the concept of sweet, juicy objects to be eaten raw or perhaps cooked. Included here are plant products that many of us think of more as nuts (*e.g.* the cashew) or raw products for drinks, both alcoholic (curaçao, eau de Creole) and non-alcoholic (coffee, chocolate).

Spices, too, are produced in quantity in the Caribbean. Sometimes they are parts of fruits such as nutmeg and mace, while others may be made from bark (cinnamon) and parts of buds (cloves). Others yield the base for pickles, insect repellents, chewing gum and even ingredients for Angostura Bitters and Worcestershire Sauce. What cannot be adequately described are the rich and varied flavours. I remember asking a friend what a star apple tasted like but no words could have prepared me for the totally unique (and delicious) flavour that greeted me when I first ate one. The same thing could be said for many of the fruits included here, so we urge you to try as many as possible.

Diversity of origin

The trees and shrubs described in this book constitute a view of West Indian history. We see some of those which have been native to the region since before man arrived in the islands perhaps as long ago as 10 000 BC and certainly no later than 2000 BC. These early hunter-gatherers are unlikely to have intentionally introduced plants, but the later invasions by Arawaks from South America about 0 AD certainly brought cassava. Desmond Nicholson[1] is of the opinion that they also introduced at least three of the trees listed in this book (Paw-paw, Soursop and Genip) as well as peanut, pineapple, cotton and tobacco and maybe others. With the next wave of arrivals came, at first, the Spanish, rapidly followed by other Europeans. The agricultural exchange between native America and Europe has been, of course, huge and complex. Most emphasis has been put on those items which passed from west to east, particularly focusing on potatoes, maize, tobacco and tomatoes. But much moved in the opposite direction and this book cites a number of *Citrus* that were probably introduced by the Spanish, although they may have themselves have first obtained these in Asia. The French are credited with introducing coffee to the region, although it is thought by many that most of the West Indies' coffee plants are descended from seedlings first raised by the Dutch in the Amsterdam Botanical Garden. The infamous Captain Bligh brought not only Breadfruit but is also credited with the Ackee and the Malay Apple. He was first commissioned to bring Breadfruit from Tahiti to the Caribbean in 1787 but, en route in the South Pacific, his crew mutinied against his supposedly brutal command. He and other officers were set adrift in an open boat but managed to survive 47 days at sea and, having travelled

3 618 nautical miles, made landfall in the Indonesian island of Timor. The mutineers sailed on to the Pitcairn Islands (which had not at this time been discovered by Europeans) where they settled and where their descendants still live. The eventual introduction of breadfruit had to wait until Bligh's second expedition in 1793. Another naval introduction to the Caribbean carries the name of its importer. This is the Shaddock, after Captain Shaddock who, in 1693, introduced the seed of this *Citrus* species previously know as the pommelo and grown in South-East Asia. By 1722 the French priest, Labat, noted huge shaddock trees being grown as shade plants in Barbados.

Other European-inspired introductions came by roundabout routes: the Star Fruit from China via Brazil, the Natal Plum from South Africa via Florida. Cocoa is of Central American origin but was not in the Caribbean in pre-Columbian times. The Spanish brought a variety of this plant called Criollo to Trinidad in 1625, but in the middle of the eighteenth century the Dutch introduced a second variety, the Amelonado, with a much darker colour and more astringent flavour. Since then, a range of hybrids have arisen between these two varieties, some of them naturally, some of them by deliberate crossing followed by selection for improved varieties. The nutmeg tree is another important commercial crop, especially in Grenada. Originally native to the East Indies, where in the sixteenth century its production was under the strict control of the Dutch, some plants were stolen by the French in what we would now call an undercover operation. These were established first in the French territories in the Indian Ocean and only later brought to Trinidad and St Vincent from where they were moved to many other islands.

Taken overall, the trees in this book include representatives of virtually all the tropical areas of the world (although I suspect there are no native Australian species here – the Cassurina is perhaps that country's best-known introduction into the Caribbean).

What's in a name?

Humans have a great desire to name things and sort them into some sort of order. For the scientific community, the Great Organiser was Carolus Linnaeus (1707–1778), a Swedish Professor at the University of Uppsala. His great contribution to classifying the living world was to propose that all creatures should be given two names (the so-called binomial nomenclature). The first name is that of the **genus** (*pl.* **genera**) and the second that of the **species**. According to the fashion of the time these names have Latin forms – in the eighteenth century Latin was the intellectual *lingua franca*. Genera usually contain a number of closely related species and are themselves grouped with other related genera into families. This grouping of like with like continues through families, orders, classes, phyla and kingdoms. The scientific names used in this book (together with the common names) illustrate the utility of this approach. For example, *Citrus sinensis* is a species of the genus *Citrus* and has the common name, Orange or Sweet Orange. *Citrus nobilis*[2] is another species of the same genus (commonly called the tangerine) and altogether this book includes nine species in this genus. Likewise there are some six species of *Annona* included. As mentioned above, the genera are grouped with other similar ones into families. The family name is listed by each entry so you can see that the *Citrus* belongs to the family Rutaceae while *Annona* is a member of the family Annonaceae. The great advantage of this naming system is that it is universal: all scientists worldwide use the same name for the same species (although arguments do break out occasionally) and newly-described species have to have their details published in suitable scientific journals. Another advantage is that it is a 'natural' classification system: that is to say, closely-related organisms appear close together in the heirarchy rather than being sorted on more arbitrary features such as size or colour. All entries in the book are listed alphabetically by family.

Of course this is all very well for the trained biologist but most of the people first settling or working in the Caribbean lacked these skills. Coming as they did from various counties of origin, they named plants largely on the basis of similarity to those of their homeland or on the basis of their appearance. So we have the Barbados Cherry which is neither a cherry (in the scientific sense) nor confined to Barbados. The Sea Grape is not related to the true grape, although there are superficial similarities, nor is that most delicious of bananas really a fig, despite its name. Worse still the isolation of populations in different islands has led to some plants being given different names in different islands – try buying the afore-mentioned figs in Antigua and you will be greeted with a blank look by the fruit vendor (but she'll gladly sell you Lady Fingers). Likewise the same name can be given to very different fruits so that the Ackee of Jamaica produces the curd-like vegetable often eaten with salt-fish, while in Barbados the name refers to a completely different fruit known in most of the Caribbean as the Genip. Denis Adams has commented on how these local names, perhaps based on a resemblance to a plant from home, can even be potentially harmful. He writes: 'Wild plants used in folk medicine are often euphemistically named when their therapeutic value is nil. Their properties may be only inferred because their names, such as Mint, Sage, or Balm, have been given to plants with a superficial resemblance to European ones, but with totally different, maybe poisonous, constituents.'[3]

Despite the pitfalls and problems that common names pose, they have undoubted charm and very often tell one something of the tree's economic importance, for example, the 'Candlenut' and the 'Hog Plum'. The 'Dead Rat Tree' graphically describes the appearance of the tree in fruit. The various fruits with 'custard' in their name are sure to have a certain sort of texture and the names of the 'Star Fruit' and 'Star Apple' are easy to understand when you eat them. Although 'Ugli Fruit' is easy enough to appreciate, 'Governor's Plum' is more enigmatic. Other names are wonderfully evocative. Those readers of V. S. Naipaul's *A House for Mr Biswas* will probably not be able to see the name 'Bay Rum Tree' without remembering the use of its oil in Mrs Tulsi's claustrophobic home. 'Sharma … undid the bandage, undid Mrs Tulsi's hair, parted it in several places, poured bay rum into her palms and from there into the partings. She worked the bay rum into Mrs Tulsi's scalp and the soaked hair squelched. Mrs Tulsi looked comforted.'

Collections

In various places in this book you will see reference to several of the botanical and other gardens scattered throughout the Caribbean. These have played, and continue to play, a vital role in conserving collections of West Indian plants. In character and origin they vary enormously, but all make a contribution to understanding how the Caribbean flora has come to be what it is today.

Many of the estates such as this one in Grenada have grown a range of fruit and spice trees since the early days of European settlement

The history of Caribbean gardening, including some of the more applied aspects, has been described by Collett and Bowe[4]. Private gardens of considerable size and complexity were to be found in the islands as early as the middle of the eighteenth century, by which time the fashion had shifted from a formal style to one where the layout contained curving walkways and more informal planting. There was much encouragement from the mother countries to improve and diversify agriculture and horticulture and the first display collection of applied botany was established in 1765 by the Governor of St Vincent, General Melville. He and other plant importers were much influenced and encouraged by the British Royal Society of Arts. It was this Society that initiated Bligh's eventual introduction of the Breadfruit. At the present time many of these 'official' botanical gardens survive: Jamaica still has 13 – some small, others, such as Hope Gardens, of considerable size (200 acres). Because of their age, these gardens often contain impressive trees of great size, that in Port of Spain, Trinidad, being a good example. Some have been neglected, others are now well cared for, but all are worth a visit. Private gardens also still flourish on many of the islands and are often open to the public. Of course these usually emphasise floral aspects of gardening rather than fruit production, but they will often contain a sample of the trees mentioned in this book. It is always worthwhile asking the gardeners (especially the older ones) about the fruit trees, but be prepared for a long conversation. Like gardeners worldwide they will have plenty to tell you.

Memories

For many people, fruit trees will conjure up memories of Caribbean holidays, of times when one lived in the region or of particular times and places. All of us will have our own particular favourites. For me there are many, not all of them totally pleasant. For instance, I recall our family's first months in Barbados and the paw-paw tree that yielded one big fruit a day. Each one was enough to feed us all at breakfast, but, oh how tired we got of it after about six months! In the end, our children rebelled and demanded some other sort of fruit (even though it had to be bought!). It was some months before I could really enjoy paw-paw again, although now when I go back again it's the first thing I want for breakfast. Avocados, too, gave us a hard time one year. I was given them each day by a colleague who had a large tree. At the beginning of the season my wife and I liked to have a whole one each. However, as the days and weeks passed, we began to find ourselves fuller and fuller from this indulgence until we realised that our early season specimens had imperceptibly grown until now these mid-season giants were two or three times as big as the first ones. No wonder we struggled.

A family banana plant can produce a serious glut as the whole stem ripens at once

Banana growing also had its particular interest. We had only a couple of trees with their junior suckers so that for months we would have no crop. Then, overnight, one had perhaps 150 bananas to eat within a few days. Gluttony, friends and a bulk-baking of banana bread prevented the ignominy of wasting any. Our coconut tree carried a crop we couldn't reach, but every couple of months a battered pick-up would arrive and a young lad would swarm up to release the ones worth having on the basis of one for us and three for him – a good bargain we thought!

The other sorts of fruit I remember are those that the students that I taught used to bring in with them and eat in laboratory practical classes (much against the safety regulations). Every week or two it was something different and of course all of them gleaned from roadside trees and bushes or growing on patches of wasteland. Genips always were popular and had a long season, guavas did well too. Golden apples I regarded as hardly worthwhile (students will eat anything) but my introduction to tamarinds has left me with a love of their sweet-but-tart 'stickinesses'. Barbados Cherries however were always a bit too acid for me – perhaps the students were too impatient to leave them until they were really ripe.

Fruits and health

The Barbados cherry is a good example of a fruit with potential. It is said to have the highest vitamin C content per gram of any fruit and there have been attempts at commercial production. Perhaps it just needs luck (or skill) in marketing to become fashionable enough to appear in the health food shops of New York and London. Although perhaps less obvious, I am sure the potential exists to develop the health-giving, perhaps even curative, properties of a number of the less well known Caribbean fruits. Many of them are, or have been used in herbal remedies, as can be seen from the descriptions in this book. Equally, there are many smaller plants not included here that feature in the region's folk medicine. In total, the Caribbean flora offers a large number of candidates for systematic investigation. Some plants have been used for so long with apparent benefit that, surely, there are active constituents that could be isolated. At a time when alternative medical treatments are becoming more popular, it is important that the traditional knowledge about how these plants and their products have been used must not be lost. However, in many cases, time is running out as it is so often the older people who have this knowledge and there is the chance that much of it will disappear with them unless interest is reactivated and folk remedies documented. Throughout the Caribbean I sense that there is an increasing interest and certainly one sees more and more books and pamphlets about medicinal plants and their uses, but there is still much to do by way of information collection. That, however, is only the start for, if we are to make the best of these plants, well regulated societies are going to have to demand that the purity and activity of the materials are guaranteed, that there is a known scientific basis of action and that the nature of possible side effects are quantified and understood. Nonetheless, books like this present one will draw attention to the less well-known plants and point to those which may warrant further investigation.

More than anything I hope this book will provoke interest and enthusiasm about West Indian fruit trees and their products. Wherever you go there will be something to look out for, either on the market stalls, in the formal gardens and more casual back-yards or even in the hedgerows and wasteland. Good hunting and good tasting.

Alick Jones

Notes

1   H Multer, M Weiss and D Nicholson (1986) *Antigua: Reefs, Rocks and Highroads of History*, Leeward Islands Science Associates, Antigua.
2   Linnaean names are conventionally printed in italics with the name of the genus having a capital initial letter, but with the species name beginning with a lower case letter.
3   C Dennis Adams (1976) *Caribbean Flora*, Nelson Carribean.
4   Jill Collett and Patrick Bowe (1998) *Gardens of the Caribbean*, Macmillan Education.

Anacardium
Occidentale Cashew, Cashew Nut, Cashew Apple

The Cashew is indigenous to Central America and the Caribbean. It is found growing wild on many of the West Indian islands. It is a medium-sized tree growing to about 40 feet with leathery, oval leaves which are about 4 ins (10 cm) long. Clusters of creamy white flowers appear at the end of the new branches, followed two months later by the strange, either bright yellow or red, pear-shaped fruit with a kidney-shaped nut appearing at the end of the fruit. The nut is the most important part of the fruit and is rich in vitamin B and protein. However, the shell of the nut contains astringent oils which can cause blistering, so the nuts are roasted before consumption to burn off these oils. The fruit itself is widely used in jams, jellies, and preserves and cooked whole, while the juice is often used in drinks for its refreshing flavour. The yellow fruits are reputedly sweeter than the red and are used to make jellies. Cashew, like many trees belonging to the Anacardiaceae family, produces a resinous sap that can blister. However, this caustic oil has its uses: years ago it was used to protect valuable, wooden antiques against ants and termites. Today, the oils are still used in linoleum and paints. Many parts of the tree and fruit have medicinal purposes and the bark contains tannin.

Mangifera indica
Mango

Native to India, where it is known as the 'King of Fruits', Captain Cook brought the Mango to Barbados from Brazil in the middle of the eighteenth century. It rapidly spread throughout the Caribbean and can be seen growing on all the islands, along the roadsides, in gardens, large and small, and in the mountains (although they do not usually bear fruit at high altitudes). A large, well-shaped tree, the Mango may reach over 100 ft (30 m) in Asia, but rarely reaches above 60 ft (18 m) in the Caribbean. The narrow, new leaves are a pinkish red, becoming dark green, leathery and glossy with maturity and having a turpentine-like odour when crushed. When flowering, the tree is covered in small, pinkish white, upright clusters of flowers which do not all set. Although the shape, colour and size of the Mango fruit vary, the reddish-green, kidney-shaped fruit is the most common. As the varieties vary, so does the flesh, from very fibrous, where only the juice is of any consequence, to smooth with a firm custard-like consistency. The delicious, yellowish-orange flesh is very sweet and juicy when ripe, with a large fibrous stone in the middle. Mangos are used in jams, jellies, desserts and juices whilst the green mango is used widely in chutneys. The best way to eat a mango is in the sea as they are a little messy! The skin of the mango contains a sap which can cause blistering to the people who may be allergic to it. However, the resinous gum and bark are used medicinally as an astringent.

Mango (*Mangifera indica*)

Schinus molle
Peppercorn Tree, Mastic Tree

The Peppercorn Tree is a native of South America. Growing readily in sandy soils, it can be found on many of the northern islands of the Caribbean. It is a common tree in the Bahamas. This evergreen tree grows to about 50 ft (15 m) and produces clusters of tiny yellowish flowers from the tips and leaf axils which are followed, on the female trees only, by long clusters of round, rosy peppercorns. These are not the principal peppercorns of commerce, but are often ground and mixed with other blends. They are often found in packets of whole peppercorns, being the little red ones.

Spondias cytherea
Ambarella, Jew Plum, Golden Apple

The Ambarella is indigenous to Polynesia. Captain Bligh brought it to Jamaica in the late eighteenth century, where it is called the Jew Plum. Probably the most widely cultivated of the Spondias, this elegant tree grows to about 60 ft (18 m) high with large leaves 8–12 ins (5–7 cm) long. Clusters of small, white flowers appear in large, loose panicles. The fruit, which hangs in clusters of four to ten, are 2–3 inches long, golden in colour with a fairly thick skin. The firm, pale yellow flesh is very juicy, sticking firmly to the large oval seed which is covered in bristle-like spines. The fruit has a sweet-acid taste and is quite difficult to eat, due to the spiky seed that the flesh clings to. Although larger than other Spondias, the fruits of the Ambarella are not usually as pleasant tasting as the choice Imbus or Red Mombins. The Ambarella is very popular with children who eat it straight off the tree. Juice can be made from the ripe fruit but with some difficulty. The almost-ripe fruits make good jams and jellies.

Ambarella (*Spondias cytherea*)

Spondias lutea
Yellow Mombin, Hog Plum, Mombin, Prune Mombin, Jobo

Originally from South America, the Yellow Mombin is generally considered inferior to the Red Mombin. The tree has not been widely cultivated, but is planted as a shade tree for animals and grows wild throughout the tropical regions. The name Hog Plum occurred in the West Indies as pigs were often tied under a Yellow Mombin for the shade and they became very fond of the fruit. The tall, stately tree grows to about 60 ft (18 m) with a thick, corky trunk and a dense, leafy crown. Terminal panicles of yellowish-white flowers are followed by clusters of orange-coloured fruits. The fruit is about 1 inch long, round, with a thin skin and an oblong seed. The yellow, soft flesh is very juicy and slightly acid. The fruit is usually eaten fresh although, having a very strong flavour, it makes very good jams and jellies. The Yellow Mombin is reputed to have many medicinal uses and teas to treat diarrhoea, gargles and poultices are all made from the leaves. The wood is used as a cork substitute and for charcoal.

Yellow Mombin (*Spondias lutea*)

Spondias mombin
Red Mombin, Spanish Plum, Jocote, Mombin

The Red Mombin comes from South America and now grows throughout the Caribbean. It is a very important fruit in Mexico and, although used quite extensively in Cuba, it is not very popular on the other islands. The spreading tree has a thick trunk and grows to about 25 ft (7.5 m). The shiny, green, oblong leaves are 5–8 ins (12–20 cm) long. Clusters of small, maroon-coloured flowers are followed by the fruits, borne singly or in clusters, which are variable in shape and size. The Red Mombin fruit is usually round, 2 ins (5 cm) long and ranges in colour from orange to deep red and is generally held to be superior to the Yellow Mombin. The flesh is plum-like, quite acid with a large, rough seed in the middle. The fruit may be eaten fresh or cooked. The cooked fruit is often dried and can be kept like this for a long time.

Red Mombin (*Spondias mombin*)

Spondias tuberosa
Imbu

Originally from South America, and now growing wild in the Caribbean, the Imbu reaches about 40 ft (12 m) with a well-shaped, low, spreading crown, often 25 ft (7.5 m) wide, and over-sized swollen roots. The small white flowers are borne in clusters 5–6 ins (12–15 cm) long. The fruit is produced on slender stems towards the end of the branches. Resembling a greengage, the oval fruit is $1\frac{1}{2}$ ins (4 cm) long and greenish-yellow in colour with a thick, tough skin. The soft flesh is sweet and slightly acid, a little like a sweet orange. If eaten before it is ripe, the flesh is very acid. The Imbu produces a mass of fruit, covering the ground under the tree when they start falling and making a very pretty picture from far away. Unfortunately, when you get closer, you come across the flies that are also attracted to the fruits. The Imbu is eaten raw or used for jams and jellies.

Annona cherimola
Cherimoya, Custard Apple, Anona

The Cherimoya originated in the mountain valleys of Peru and Ecuador and has now found its way into the Caribbean. It is not found as often as the Custard Pale, with which it is often confused. A deciduous, shrubby tree growing to about 20 ft (6 m) high and preferring higher elevations, it is not found near the coast. The dull, green leaves vary in size from tree to tree. The yellowish green, highly-scented flowers appear at the end of the branches. The fruits vary in shape and size but are usually a conical, heart-shape. The delicate, green skin is made up of what look like, overlapping scales. Inside, the white custard-like flesh, is smooth and delicious with a banana or pineapple flavour. The Cherimoya is becoming popular throughout the world but, because of its delicate nature, it is a difficult fruit to export. It is quite often made into desserts. However, the fruit is so good, it should be spooned out of the skin and eaten fresh.

Cherimoya (*Annona cherimola*)

Annona glabra
Alligator Apple, Cork-wood, Custard Apple, Pond Apple

Native to the West Indies and Central America, the Pond Apple tree can eventually grow to 40 ft (12 m), but is usually seen as a small evergreen with oblong, glossy green leaves about 4 ins (10 cm) long. It grows best in swampy areas, hence the name Pond Apple Tree. The large flowers have creamy white petals with flashes of dark red in the centre. The conical or heart-shaped fruit is 3–5 ins (8–12 cm) long with a smooth, yellowish skin. The soft, yellow flesh falls into dry, fibrous segments with brown seeds. Due to the rather unpleasant flavour, the Pond Apple is often considered poisonous, although this is not so. The fruit is mostly eaten by animals.

Annona muricata
Soursop, Guanabana, Sweetsop, Corossol

The Soursop originated in South America and is now found throughout the Caribbean. It is a very popular garden tree for the fruits it provides. The slender medium-sized tree grows to about 20 ft (6 m) with narrow, glossy leaves, 3–4 ins (8–10 cm) long. The fleshy, greenish-yellow flowers are borne directly on the trunk or branches. The large, oddly-shaped fruit has fleshy spines and a shiny, pale green skin. It can weigh up to 8 lbs (4 kg), although shape and weight vary considerably. Inside the fruit, the aromatic, white cottony, custard-like pulp has a sweet, sour flavour and contains many black seeds. The fruit is seldom eaten fresh, but usually made into custards, ice cream and refreshing drinks. It is widely used in Cuba as a drink, where the name Guanabana comes from. All parts of the Soursop Tree have been used for medicinal purposes. The leaves are often used in a refreshing drink for rashes and heat. Having insecticidal properties, the leaves are often used to ward off mosquitoes. The bark has been used for intestinal problems, although an overdose can be very dangerous.

Soursop (*Annona muricata*)

Annona reticulata
Custard Apple, Bullock's Heart, Jamaica Apple

The Custard Apple is a native of the West Indies and grows widely throughout the Caribbean. Although fairly popular in the islands, it lacks the flavour of the Sugar Apple and Cherimoya. The spreading, deciduous tree grows to about 25 ft (7.5 m), with glossy, dark green leaves. The strongly scented, yellowish-green flowers appear at the ends of the branches. The Custard Apple takes a long time to reach maturity. When ripe, the fruit is usually reddish yellow in colour and conical or heart-shaped, hence its name, Bullock's Heart. Containing numerous seeds, the flesh is creamy white with a granular consistency and is very sweet. Like all the *Annonas*, the Custard Apple also has medicinal properties. For example the seeds were pounded into a powder which was used to ward off lice and fleas.

Custard Apple (*Annona reticulata*)

Annona squamosa
Sugar Apple, Sweetsop, Bullock's Heart

The Sugar Apple is indigenous to South America and the West Indies. However, it is widely held by many that it originated in Asia. Seen in many gardens in the Caribbean, this deciduous tree rarely grows above 20 ft (6 m) high and often looks more like an overgrown shrub. The highly-scented, fleshy, greenish-yellow flowers grow in the axils of the leaves. The knobbly-skinned fruits are green, having a rounded, heart shape. They are about 4–5 ins (10–12 cm) long and soft to the touch when ripe. The fruit easily breaks into sections, each section containing a black seed. The delicious flesh is creamy white, slightly granular and very sweet. Although often considered sickly sweet by many, children usually love it. The Sugar Apple is probably the best known of the *Annonas* in the Caribbean and, like most of the them, the Sugar Apple has medicinal qualities. Teas, using the leaves, were often brewed to help with gynaecological problems.

Sugar Apple (*Annona squamosa*)

Carissa macrocarpa
Natal Plum, Carissa

The Natal Plum originated in South Africa and was introduced into Florida in the nineteenth century and it has now found its way into many of the islands. Although usually referred to as a shrub, it will grow to about 20 ft (6 m). Widely used by landscapers for its dense foliage and spreading habit, the Natal Plum can often be found in hotel grounds. The tree usually forms many branches which, together with its thorns, make for a very good hedge. The dense, shiny, dark green leaves and small, white, jasmine-like flowers are followed by small, red plums. The fruits vary widely in shape (round or oblong), size and flesh. The ripe fruit has a papery skin with red flesh and a milky-white latex containing little black seeds. When handling the fruit, the milky sap will stick to your fingers and is quite difficult to remove. The sweet, acidic fruit can be eaten raw, but it is fairly tart and is therefore used mostly in jellies and pies.

Natal Plum (*Carissa macrocarpa*)

Crescententia cujete
Calabash

The Calabash is native to the West Indies, Central and South America. It is an evergreen tree growing to about 30 ft (9 m), with long, thin, spreading branches covered entirely by small clusters of light green leaves attached by short stems. Although not a very elegant tree, orchid growers are very fond of having a Calabash tree in the garden as epiphytic orchids and bromeliads

grow very well on it. Tiny green, beadlike buds appear directly on the branches which open into papery, greyish-yellow, bell-shaped flowers. Pollinated by bats, the flowers are only open for one night. The bright green, round or oblong fruits, which can be up to 15 ins (38 cm) in diameter, have a very hard, woody, waterproof shell and are full of white pulp containing seeds. The fruits turn a yellowish-brown when ripe and are often tied when young to force them to grow into a useful shape. Although edible, the pulp is not very pleasant and not used much as a food, although years ago it was eaten raw to help expel the placenta from the womb after childbirth and is still used as a purgative. The hard, wooden shell has many uses. As a child I can remember them in the kitchen: the goat's milk was always collected in a calabash and no fishing boat ever went out without a calabash to bail out sea water. The hard shells have been used to make musical instruments for many years and are still used today to make maracas.

Calabash (*Crescententia cujete*)

Bixa orellana
Annatto, Arnotto, Lipstick Tree

The *Bixa orellana*, which is often called the Lipstick Tree because of the orange henna or annatto dye that comes out of the seeds, is native to tropical America. Often seen growing as a large shrub, it has heart-shaped leaves about 3–7 ins (8–18 cm) long. Terminal clusters of pink or white flowers appear, rather like cherry blossom, followed by the bright red or brown, fattish, almond-shaped seedpods, about 2 ins (5 cm) long and covered in short, soft spines. These pods split open naturally, revealing between 40 and 50 seeds covered in a bright red, waxy coating. *Bixa orellana* was used by the Indians for skin dyes and is now grown commercially and sold as annatto

for the yellow dye obtained from the seeds. Annatto dye is essentially tasteless making it a useful colouring agent in fruit juices and processed foods. Before the rigid controls of today, it was often added to margarine to give it the appearance of butter!

Annatto (*Bixa orellana*)

BOMBACEAE

Durio zibethinus
Durian

The Durian is best known for its unpleasant smell, which is a shame, as the fruit is delicious. Originally from the Malayan region, the Durian is occasionally found in the West Indies, although not in too many gardens as the smell usually attracts flies and other insects. The tree grows to about 65 ft (19.5 m) and has oblong leaves, 6–7 ins (15–18 cm) long, with a leathery, shiny surface. The white, bell-shaped flowers appear in clusters on the branches followed by the green, oval fruit, 6–8 ins (15–20 cm) long, covered with short, woody spines. Europeans do not usually like the fruit, because of the unpleasant odour, but the creamy, brown, custard-like pulp is delicious.

Adansonia digitata
Baobab Tree, Dead Rat Tree, Monkey Bread Tree, Sour Gourd

Baobab Tree (*Adansonia digitata*)

A large tree native to Africa, the Baobab Tree was brought to the West Indies for its religious and medicinal qualities. It is one of the longest-living trees and one of Africa's most important trees. As the trunk ages, it collects huge amounts of water. It is a slow growing tree with a massive, spongy, squat trunk and small branches. The common name, Dead Rat Tree, comes from the way the fruits hang on very thin branches and which, from a distance, look much like dead rats. The edible fruit contains a yellowish-white pulp, rich in tartaric acid, and is often used as a seasoning. The rather mealy flesh contains many seeds having many medicinal properties. The bark is used for making rope.

BORAGINACEAE

Cordia collococca
Wild Clammy Cherry

The Wild Clammy Cherry is found throughout the Caribbean. It is a pretty, spreading ornamental tree growing to 30 ft (9 m). It has small leaves. The fruit follows clusters of small white flowers. The bright red shiny little fruits are like a cherry with a sticky fleshy pulp. The Wild Clammy Cherry has many medicinal uses, including the use of the leaves in a hot tea as a soporific.

Wild Clammy Cherry (*Cordia collococca*)

Cordia dentata
Clam and Cherry, White Manjack, Jackwood

This small ornamental tree, which grows throughout the Caribbean, is mostly seen on roadsides. The White Manjack grows to about 30 ft (9 m) high with rough, green leaves about 4 ins (10 cm) long. Large clusters of small, white flowers are followed by hanging clusters of small, greenish white berries, rather like redcurrants. The white flesh has a sticky consistency which is very popular with children. They are, however, messy garden trees.

Clam and Cherry (*Cordia dentata*)

Cordia sebestena
Geranium Tree, Geiger Tree

The Geranium Tree is native to the West Indies and is seen throughout the Caribbean growing along the roadsides and in many gardens. Mostly grown as an ornamental, the tree flowers throughout the year. It is small, growing to about 30 ft (9 m) high, with rough, stiff, dark green 7 in (18 cm) long leaves. Four or five trumpet-shaped flowers appear in clusters. These are a bright orangey-red in colour and about 1 in (2.5 cm) in diameter. The small, greenish white berries which follow are edible but very gluey. The wood is used in furniture making.

CARICACEAE

Carica papaya
Paw-paw, Papaya

The Paw-paw, or Papaya, has been around for many centuries, probably brought by the Spanish to the Caribbean from South America. Although the Paw-paw is described as a tree, this is not strictly so, as the trunk is fibrous and pulpy and not a hard wood. This rapidly-growing specimen will grow to about 30 ft (9 m) with large leaves about 3 ft (1 m) long which leave a scar on the trunk when they fall off. The 'tree' will develop one of three types of flowers: the male being a small white flower on a long stem; the female,

usually a larger flower in single or cluster form, or the hermaphrodite flower. The fruit can vary in colour and size, from orange to a deep pinkish-coral. It also varies in size from large, up to 15 lbs (8 kg), down to the small pear-shaped fruits favoured by the commercial markets. Most parts of the 'tree' contain the enzyme papain, which is used extensively in commercial tenderisers. Tough meat is often layered between slices of green paw-paw or cooked in the leaves. The sweet, juicy flesh has a smooth consistency with a mass of small greyish-black seeds encased in jelly. With a squeeze of lime, the Paw-paw is a common breakfast delight. The green fruit is used as a vegetable on many of the islands. Medicinally, the juice of the leaves, roots and 'trunk' has been used to aid various skin disorders.

Paw-paw (*Carica papaya*)

Terminalia catappa
West Indian Almond, Almond Tree, Indian Almond

The Almond Tree, or Indian Almond comes from Malaysia, and now makes its appearance in most tropical regions. Often seen around hotels and public beach areas, it thrives in sandy conditions and stands up well to wind. The tree will grow to about 50 ft (15 m) with widely spreading branches. The large, round, glossy green leaves are about 8 ins (20 cm) long, becoming leathery and turning red with maturity. The small, white flowers are followed by green, almond-shaped fruit. These are about 2 ins (5 cm) long. When ripe, they fall off the tree and turn brown exposing the fibrous husk which contains the seed. A favourite pastime with children is to pound the husk with a stone in order to reach the delicious little 'almond' inside. There is no easy way to get these 'almonds' out, so they are not much used in cooking, unless you are willing to spend hours pounding!

Almond Tree (*Terminalia catappa*)

Dillenia indica
Elephant Apple

The Elephant Apple originally came from India, but it now grows in most of the tropical regions of the world and can be seen throughout the Caribbean. It is an elegant, short-trunked tree, growing to about 30 ft (9 m), with very distinctive leaves. These have strong, straight veins running through the leaves, giving the impression of finely pleated material. The flowers, which appear under the leaves, have five large petals surrounding a mass of yellow stamens. The green fruits follow, looking as though they have a covering of overlapping petals. In fact, these are the sepals surrounding the fruit, which is round and about the size of a large orange. The sepals are used in curries and the fruit is edible but not much used.

Elephant Apple (*Dillenia indica*)

Diospyros digyna
Black Sapote

The Black Sapote is probably native to the Philippines, although it is widely thought that it may be indigenous to Mexico. Although called Black Sapote, it has no relationship to the Sapote, but is related to the oriental Persimmon (*Kaki*), and is often referred to as the 'Black Persimmon'. The Black Sapote is not grown commercially in the West Indies but can be found in some of the older gardens. It is a well-shaped tree with a rounded crown which can reach 50–60 ft (15–18 m) in good soil. However, it is more often seen as a medium-sized tree. The tree has dark brown bark and bright, shiny, oblong leaves, 4–7 ins (10–18 cm) long. Small, white flowers are followed by the round, flattish fruit about 3–4 ins (8–10 cm) in diameter with a greenish brown skin. It is difficult to know when the fruit is ripe as the skin does not change colour with ripening. The unfortunate, dark chocolate-coloured flesh is not very eye-catching. However, with a little lime or orange juice, the sweet fruit becomes quite pleasant to the taste. The flesh freezes very well so it can be used in many dessert recipes and, of course, it makes wonderful ice cream.

ELAEOCACEAERPA

Muntingia calabura
Muntingia

Muntingia (*Muntingia calabura*)

The Muntingia is native to tropical America and the West Indies. This small, rapidly growing tree will reach 30 ft (9 m) high in sheltered spots. Fully grown, the tree forms an attractive, spreading, flat-topped crown with open branches, making it a popular garden ornamental. Small, white flowers appear on slender stems growing out of the leaf axils, followed by the fruit. These berries are white or pink, sweet, about $\frac{1}{2}$ in (1 cm) in diameter, containing a juicy pulp with many minute seeds. Birds are attracted to the fruit, so you will have to be on your guard if you want to collect them for jellies and jams. The Muntingia fruit is very high in ascorbic acid (vitamin C).

EUPHORBIACEAE

Aleurites moluccana
Candlenut

Candlenut (*Aleurites moluccana*)

The Candlenut, a native of Malaysia, is now found on most of the islands of the Caribbean. The tree grows to about 60 ft (18 m) high with evergreen leaves 2–5 ins (5–12 cm) long. The young leaves have a dusting of white powder, giving a silvery sheen to the tree from a distance. The small, white flowers appear in large, open panicles followed by the fruit, which is brownish-grey in colour. This is about 2 ins (5 cm) wide and contains one or two hard-shelled black seeds. In the past, the white kernels were occasionally used in cooking, but were mostly used to obtain oil for lamps and candles, hence the name Candlenut. Today, the nuts are mostly used in bead-making.

Hippomane mancinella
Manchineel

The fruit of the Manchineel is definitely <u>not</u> edible. I am including it here as many visitors to the Caribbean are unaware of its dangers. A native of the Caribbean and Central America, the Manchineel grows to about 50 ft (15 m) high and has a pale grey bark. The shiny, pale green leaves are 3 ins (8 cm) long. The inconspicuous green flowers can be either male or female. The resulting round, green fruit, resembling a greengage, are extremely poisonous. A milky sap, produced by the Manchineel, can cause severe blistering. The tree can be found on most of the islands and unfortunately many of the beaches are still fringed with Manchineel trees, although hotels

are usually careful in having them removed. The small fruits are often seen rolling around in the surf and care should be taken that children do not pick them up. Don't be tempted to shelter under a Manchineel in a rainstorm as the resin will be washed off the leaves and fall onto your skin resulting in blistering. I remember, years ago, staying in a small cottage in the Grenadines, where the toilet seat had been made out of Manchineel wood. Unfortunately, it took us a long time to find out what was causing the resulting blistering! We never found out who had made the unfortunate seat!

Manchineel (*Hippomane mancinella*)

Phyllantrus acidus
Gooseberry Tree, Otaheite Gooseberry, West Indian Gooseberry, Wild Plum

Native to tropical Asia and the East Indies, the Gooseberry Tree was introduced to the West Indies in the late eighteenth century. Seen on most of the islands, it is usually planted as an ornamental. It is a small, spreading tree growing to about 20 ft (6 m) high, with alternate, softish, bright green leaves up to 3 ins (8 cm) long. The new leaves have a pink tinge to them. Clusters of small, pink to reddish flowers appear along the edges of slender branches hiding amongst the leaves. The ribbed grape-sized fruits hang in clusters along the branches. The yellowish-white, crisp, juicy, rounded berries about $\frac{3}{4}$ in (2 cm) in diameter, are highly acidic. The Gooseberry makes very good jelly, which will be red in colour. They also make a good pie and although the fruits can be eaten raw, they are very tart.

Gooseberry Tree (*Phyllantrus acidus*)

FLACOURTIACEAE

Dovyalis caffra
Kei Apple, Umkokolo

More of a shrub than a tree, the Kei Apple is native to South Africa, but is found in some parts of the Caribbean where it is often grown as a hedge or an ornamental. Related to the Ceylon Gooseberry (*Dovyalis hebecarpa*), the spreading little tree is densely covered with dark green, glossy leaves which are about 2 ins (5 cm) long. There are sharp thorns on the trunk and branches. The male and female flowers appear on separate trees but neither has petals. The apple-shaped fruit is 1 in (2.5 cm) in diameter, with a thin, slightly furry skin, bright golden yellow in colour. The aromatic flesh is acid and very juicy. Unless very ripe, the fruit is extremely acid and is used far more in making jams and jellies than it is eaten raw.

Dovyalis hebecarpa
Ceylon Gooseberry, Ketemilla

The Ceylon Gooseberry, as the name would imply, comes from Ceylon (Sri Lanka) and India. The shrubby tree will grow to about 20 ft (6 m), although, the more tropical the conditions, the taller it will grow. The Ceylon Gooseberry is found on some of the islands and grows well in Cuba. The tree has spiny thorns on the trunk and carries wide-spreading branches which tend to become pendulous when fruiting. The young leaves are pale green and slightly furry, becoming oval, tough, 2–4 ins (5–10 cm) long and dark green with maturity. The fruit is the same shape and size as its cousin the Kei (*Dovylis caffra*) but is a deep maroon in colour with a more furry skin. Inside, the purplish flesh is sweet, but very acid, with a gooseberry-like flavour. Although eaten raw it makes very good jams and jellies and is often eaten with meat and fish.

Flacourtia ramontchi
Ramontchi, Governor's Plum

The Governor's Plum, as it is called on most of the West Indian islands, is a native of India and tropical Asia. The small, shrubby tree will grow to about 25 ft (7.5 m), although it is mostly found growing in hedge form as its dense growth and thorns make it almost impenetrable. The male and female flowers appear on separate trees. Large quantities of yellowish-red, round fruits are produced on the female trees. The fruit, about 1 in (2.5 cm) in diameter, has a thin skin surrounding white, juicy, rather acid flesh containing several small seeds. The fruit is better eaten raw, as cooking releases a bitter taste from the skin. Unripe fruit is mostly used in jams and jellies.

GUTTIFERAE

Clusia rosea
Autograph Tree, Pitch Apple, Scotch Attorney

The Autograph Tree is native to the West Indies and is found throughout the Caribbean. The tree will grow to about 50 ft (15 m) in height and has thick, roundish, shiny leaves up to 8 ins (20 cm) long. The green fruits, about 3 ins (8 cm) in diameter, follow the waxy, white, magnolia-like flowers which become brown and woody with maturity. As it is fairly well known that the leaves will accept 'autographs', most trees in public places have well-named leaves, hence the name Autograph Tree. The Spanish also used the leaves for writing paper when such things were very scarce. The wood is used for furniture. The bark and fruit have many medicinal purposes.

Autograph Tree (*Clusia rosea*)

Garcinia dulcis
Gourka

The Gourka, a native of India, is occasionally found in the Caribbean – there are a few trees in some of the older gardens of Puerto Rico. A small, well-shaped tree growing to about 20 ft (6 m), it has large, pointed, narrow leaves about 6 ins (15 cm) long. The small, greenish-white flowers appear on short stems directly on the branches. The roundish fruits have a very juicy, acidic pulp containing between one and five seeds. The tree will flower and fruit on and off during the summer. Not often eaten raw, the Gourka is used in cooking and for jams and chutneys.

Gourka (*Garcinia dulcis*)

Mammea americana
Mamey, Mammee Apple, Santo Domingo Apricot

Probably one of the most elegant trees in the Caribbean, the Mammee was already growing in the islands when Columbus first visited. Generally held to be indigenous to the West Indies, the Mammee probably made its way to the islands from South America. A well-shaped tree, it grows to about 60 ft (18 m) with wide-spreading branches and dense foliage. The glossy, dark green leaves, 4–6 ins (10–15 cm) long, grow in thick clusters. Highly-scented, white flowers appear directly on the larger branches, on and off throughout the year, followed by the large, brown, leathery-skinned fruit. These are either round or oblong and can be up to 8 ins (20 cm) long. Once peeled, the firm, dense, orange flesh ranges from being slightly insipid to delicious, with a peachy-mango flavour. Each fruit contains between one and four large, rough seeds. Delicious as a fruit, the Mammee is also used to make jams, jellies and desserts. On some of the French islands the flowers are distilled to make the Eau de Creole liqueur. The wood is used fairly extensively in furniture making.

Mammee Apple (*Mammea americana*)

Garcinia mangostana
Mangosteen

If the Mango is described as the King of Fruits, the Mangosteen is the Queen, although they are not related. Often described as one of the finest fruits of the world, the Mangosteen comes from tropical Asia. It can be found on many of the islands, usually in the older gardens, although it is not as widely grown as the fruit warrants. It is a medium-sized tree growing to about 30 ft (9 m) with dark green, glossy foliage. The leathery, oblong leaves are 8–10 ins (20–25 cm) long. Red, rose-like flowers that appear on young branches are polygamous. The smallish fruits, about the size of a plum, are reddish-brown and purple in colour, with a thick, smooth skin tinged with spots. The pearly white flesh is divided into five segments surrounding flat seeds. The flesh has a grape-like consistency with a sweet, juicy, slightly acid flavour. The fruit is mostly eaten raw. In India it is used medicinally. The Mangosteen contains tannin.

LAURACEAE

Cinnamomum verum
Cinnamon

The Cinnamon originally came from India and was brought to the Caribbean centuries ago by the Spanish. The tree grows on many of the islands and can be found growing commercially in Grenada, the 'Spice Island'. Growing to about 45 ft (14 m), the tree has tough, shiny green

Cinnamon (*Cinnamomum verum*)

leaves, although when grown commercially it is usually prevented from growing too tall. Clusters of small, white flowers appear, followed by the berries. The bark of the tree is the much-prized spice, 'cinnamon'. This is stripped off the branches after two years' growth and left to ferment in the humidity. The outer surface is then scraped off, leaving the 'cleaned' bark that is sun dried and exported. Small bunches of cinnamon 'sticks' can often be found in the market and on vegetable stalls. It is usually sold commercially in powdered form. Cinnamon is widely used in the Caribbean to flavour desserts and drinks.

Persea americano
Avocado, Butter Pear, Pear, Zaboca

The Avocado has been in cultivation for centuries. Originally from Central America, it is now found in most parts of the tropics. There are many varieties of Avocado which fall into three main categories: the West Indian, with a smooth, leathery skin; the Guatemalan with a thick, rough skin, and the Mexican, which is much smaller with a soft, thin skin and spice-scented leaves. The Avocado tree usually grows to about 30 ft (9 m), but is often kept at a convenient height for picking. A graceful, well-shaped tree, it is usually fairly densely branched with dark green leaves from 5–9 ins (12–24 cm) long.

The clusters of small, greenish-white flowers profusely cover the ends of the branches, which, luckily for the tree, do not all set. The tree quite often loses its leaves before the fruit appears. These vary in shape, size and colour, depending on the variety. The flesh is greenish-yellow, having a buttery consistency, with a large seed in the middle. The Avocado, which has the highest protein value of all the fresh fruits, is also rich in vitamins and minerals and has a high oil content. Used mostly in salads, the Avocado is also delicious on its own. Having medicinal properties, the leaves are used in teas for stomach cramps.

Avocado (*Persea americano*)

Tamarindus indica
Tamarind

The Tamarind comes from India and was brought to the Caribbean some three centuries ago. It now grows throughout the islands, where it is one of the more graceful, spreading ornamentals in the region, grown both for shade and for its fruits. The tree is slow-growing, but can reach a height of 50 ft (15 m) or more. The feathery compound leaves close at night and will also close in a high wind. Being a member of the pea family, it carries flowers typical of this group. They are red and yellow and relatively large. The green, pod-like fruits turn brown and are about 6 ins (15 cm) long and very brittle when ripe. Inside the pod, an acidic, sugary pulp surrounds the seeds. Because of its sweet and sour taste, the Tamarind is used widely in cooking for sauces, drinks, chutneys, candies, jellies and curries. It is an important

ingredient of Worcestershire Sauce and appears in Angostura Bitters. You will often find the famous West Indian Tamarind Ball, a sugary confectionery, being sold along the roadsides. The Jamaicans used to export large quantities of Tamarind, stripped of their pods and packed in sugar. Many parts of the Tamarind have medicinal qualities. The wood is used in furniture making. When I was a child we were very often reminded at school of the Tamarind whips kept by the headmaster in olden times!

Tamarind (*Tamarindus indica*)

Malpighia glabra
Barbados Cherry, Acerola, West Indian Cherry

The Barbados Cherry, found in Central America, Mexico and parts of South America, is native to the West Indies. A small tree, reaching about 15 ft (4.5 m) high, it is often grown as an ornamental or hedge as it is easily pruned into an attractive shape and will produce flowers and fruit on and off throughout the year. The 2–3 in (5–8 cm)-long leaves are shiny, dark green and densely cover the tree. Small, pink flowers with a fragrant scent are followed by the fruit which are very like a cherry but with slight ridges running from top to bottom. The young, green fruit starts turning orange then dark red when ripe. Inside the very thin skin, the creamy white, acidic flesh contains three seeds. The Barbados Cherry has a very high vitamin C content and received much attention when it was found to contain more ascorbic acid than any other fruit of its size. A dried version is now sold under the name 'Acerola'. The fruits are used in jams, jellies and preserves. They are also delicious when eaten straight from the tree, but only when ripe as they are very acidic.

Barbados Cherry (*Malpighia glabra*)

Artocarpus
Breadnut, Chataigne

The Breadnut, the seeded variety of the Breadfruit, was introduced to the West Indies by the French for its likeness to the chestnut, hence the name 'chataigne'. The tree is very similar to the Breadfruit, although the female flowers are sterile and the seeds will not produce a Breadfruit tree. The fruit, which is slightly smaller than a Breadfruit, is green, round and very spiny. Inside is a mass of pulp containing the seeds, which are called 'breadnuts'. When taken out of the pulp, the seeds resemble chestnuts and I can remember the Christmas turkey being stuffed with mashed breadnuts to resemble chestnut stuffing. Breadnuts are used widely in Trinidad to accompany 'Calaloo' soup and most of the Leeward Islands have uses for the Breadnut in various stews or to accompany fish.

Breadnut (*Artocarpus*)

Artocarpus altilis
Breadfruit

The British government sent Captain Bligh to the Polynesian Islands to collect Breadfruit suckers and take them to the West Indies, intending to produce a cheap source of starchy food for the sugar plantation workers. It was on the first expedition that the mutiny on the *Bounty* occurred. The Botanical Gardens in St Vincent have a tree which they claim came from one of the original suckers. The Breadfruit is one of the most striking trees growing in the Caribbean and can be seen on most of the islands. The tree reaches a height of 40–60 ft (12–18 m) and has large, leathery, deeply-lobed leaves, sometimes as large as 3 ft (1 m) long. The flowers are male and female. The male are large, yellow and catkin-shaped while the numerous female flowers are grouped together to form a large, round head. The large green fruit appears singly or in clusters of two or three and are globular, up to 8 ins (20 cm) in diameter. They become brownish yellow as they ripen. Overripe fruits are usually thrown away as they are not fit to eat. The creamy flesh has a starchy consistency and is eaten boiled or baked, being especially delicious when eaten like a baked potato with a little butter. It is still possible to see the Breadfruit being baked on 'coalpots' and sold by the roadside in St Lucia and St Vincent. Medicinally, the leaves are boiled and made into a tea thought to reduce blood pressure. The Breadfruit tree is propagated by suckers taken off the roots at the base of the tree as it does not produce seeds. The Breadnut is the seeded variety. However, you will not grow a Breadfruit tree from one of these seeds.

Breadfruit (*Artocarpus altilis*)

Artocarpus heterophyllus
Jakfruit, Jackfruit

The strange looking Jakfruit, a relative of the Breadfruit, is another Malaysian tree found throughout the Caribbean and Central America. The tree grows to about 50 ft (15 m) high, with glossy, leathery, oval leaves about 9 ins (23 cm) long. The small yellow flowers are male and female. The male flowers appear in tiny oblong clusters 2–4 ins (5–10 cm) long, while the female flowers appear in round clusters on the same tree. The unusual fruits, which are borne directly on the trunk and larger branches, are some of the largest fruits in the world, sometimes weighing up to 70 lbs (30 kg) each, although they are usually 15–20 lbs (7–10 kg). The green, spiny, oddly-shaped fruit develops an unpleasant odour as it ripens. However, the soft, yellowish pulp is delicious with a slight banana-like flavour. It can be eaten raw or cooked and often accompanies curries. The pulp is full of numerous long, white seeds which are also good roasted or boiled. The fruit is often cooked as a vegetable just before it ripens.

Jackfruit (*Artocarpus heterophyllus*)

Musa
Figs, Lady Fingers, Silver Fingers

These tiny bananas grow in exactly the same way as the regular bananas and plantains. However, the fruits seem to have a more solid consistency and are often sweeter than the larger bananas. Most of the southern islands in the West Indies refer to these bananas as 'figs', a name which probably came from India where it was thought that Adam and Eve used banana leaves to cover themselves rather than fig leaves. Figs are very popular in the islands, and you will find them in most of the local markets. They are well worth buying but make sure they are yellow and not green. Figs are very rarely exported, so it is unlikely that you will find them outside the tropical regions.

Musa acuminata
Banana

Banana (*Musa acuminata*)

There are over 300 varieties of bananas growing throughout the tropical regions of the world. Many wild bananas exist, although these are usually inedible. 'Gross Michel' was one of the first cultivated varieties to be introduced into the Caribbean. However, susceptible to disease, it has been crossed with the hardier 'Cavendish' to produce the commercial varieties of today. The Banana is not strictly a tree, as the 'trunk' is made up of long, overlapping stems of leaves rising out of the rhizome beneath the ground. The young, paddle-shaped leaves soon become torn by the wind and they will grow up to 20 ft (6 m) long at maturity. A large, purple bud appears which opens to reveal the female, fruit-producing flowers. These flowers become fruit without fertilisation. The pollen-producing male flowers follow later. Once the stem of the Banana starts to ripen, it is cut off. By now one or two new shoots will have appeared rising out of the ground from the same rhizome – these are the new Banana 'trees'. Driving through the Banana plantations in the Caribbean, it is a common sight to see the stems of Bananas hanging in large plastic bags. This is done to prevent damage before they are exported. Bananas contain vitamins A, B and C and are high in nutritional value. Consequently, they are a common source of food throughout the world. Green bananas are often boiled and served as a vegetable. Meat and fish are often wrapped and cooked in banana leaves, securing the juices and giving a unique flavour.

Musa paradisiaca
Plantain

In its overall form, the Plantain is exactly like the Banana although sometimes the plant may be larger. It is the fruit that differs. The Plantain is one of the most important foods in the Caribbean – it is almost impossible to have a West Indian meal without Plantain, in some form, as an accompaniment. The Plantain is inedible when raw. Cooked green, it is usually boiled or baked. When ripe, it appears almost rotten, as the skin is brownish black, but the flesh is yellowish-white and sweet and in this form it is usually cut lengthwise into strips and fried. Fried Plantain is nearly always served with fish.

MYRISTRICACEAE

Myristica fragrans
Nutmeg

The Nutmeg, a native of the East Indies, was introduced into Trinidad in the early part of the nineteenth century. It did not do very well there and was taken to Grenada, the 'Spice Island', where it flourished. At that time the nutmeg trees in the East Indies were stricken with a disease which devastated their nutmeg trade leaving a big hole in the market which Grenada soon filled. Nutmeg has now become one of Grenada's largest exports, supplying nearly 50 per cent of the world's needs. The Nutmeg is a handsome tree, growing to about 50 ft (15 m), with shiny, dark green leaves. The small, white flowers are inconspicuous compared to the beautiful fruits that follow. These are like small, pale yellow apricots, which split open on the tree revealing the brown nut surrounded by the lace-like, bright red aril. All parts of the Nutmeg fruit are used – the outer fruit is made into a local brandy, the lace-like red aril is the spice known as mace and the brown seed, the important part, is ground into nutmeg powder or exported whole. Prized as a spice in the West Indies, the Nutmeg has many medicinal qualities from poultices for chest complaints to athlete's foot. Oil is extracted from the kernel and used in perfume. The Nutmeg can be found in many of the islands. St Vincent has some very good specimens in the Botanical Gardens.

Nutmeg (*Myristica fragrans*)

MYRTACEAE

Eugenia rhombea
Spiceberry, Red-berry Stopper

The Red-berry Stopper Tree is a small, erect evergreen growing to about 25 ft (7.5 m) with a flaking, greyish bark. The stiff, thick, leathery leaves are a dull, dark green on the surface and yellowish-green underneath. The white flowers form in clusters on 1 in (2.5 cm)-long stalks and are followed by the fruits. These are fleshy berries, each with one seed, starting out red and turning to almost black when ripe. The trees are found throughout the Caribbean, where the wood is often used for fence posts.

Eugenia uniflora
Surinam Cherry, Pitanga, Florida Cherry

The Surinam Cherry, known as the Pitanga in its native Brazil, can be seen growing on many of the islands. It is a very popular garden tree, often made into a hedge, where it will continue to fruit. The bushy little tree grows to about 25 ft (7.5 m) high, with dark green, highly aromatic, glossy foliage. The new growth is deep red in colour. The single white flowers are borne in the axils of the leaves. The fruit is roundish, 1 in (2.5 cm) in diameter with eight distinct ridges running from top to bottom. When ripe, the fruit is deep crimson, soft and very juicy with one large seed in the middle. The Surinam Cherry is used widely in jams and jellies, often rivalling the Guava in flavour. The leaves can be crushed to ward off flies.

Surinam Cherry (*Eugenia uniflora*)

Myrciara cauliflora
Jaboticaba

The Jaboticaba is a native of Brazil and is an attractive tree growing to about 30 ft (9 m) high with a crown of pale green foliage made up of narrow, oval leaves about 1 in (2.5 cm) long. The small, round, grape-like fruits are borne singularly or in clusters of two or three directly on the trunk and the larger branches. The fruits, which average 1 in (2.5 cm) in diameter, are dark purple, almost black when ripe, and have a tough, thin skin which covers a pinkish white, juicy, somewhat gelatinous pulp containing a few small seeds. The fruit has a pleasant grape-like flavour and is usually eaten fresh. The Jaboticaba is used frequently in wine making.

Jaboticaba (*Myrciara cauliflora*)

MYRTACEAE

Pimenta dioica
Allspice, Wholespice, Jamaica Pepper, Pimento

The Allspice Tree is native to the Caribbean and Central America and is grown widely in Jamaica and Grenada. The medium-sized tree grows to about 30 ft (9 m) high and has a smooth, greyish bark. The shiny, leathery leaves have the same spicy aroma as the seeds. The small, white flowers are followed by clusters of greenish-brown berries. These berries are picked green and then dried, becoming the 'Allspice', so named as they have the aroma of cinnamon, cloves and nutmeg. The oily leaves are often used for flavouring as well. The Allspice is often confused with its close relative, the Bay Rum Tree. Allspice is usually found, commercially, in powder form. However, it loses a lot of its flavour in this form – wherever possible, buy the dried seeds and grind them when needed. Allspice is widely used in the Caribbean for flavouring.

Psidium guajava
Guava

The native home of the Guava is tropical America, although it has been in the Caribbean for many centuries. A fast growing tree reaching about 25 ft (7.5 m) high, the Guava is not a very attractive garden tree as it has untidy branches. The leaves are light green and 3–6 ins (8–15 cm) long. Creamy-white flowers sit in clusters amongst the leaves, followed by the fruits three months later. The Guava fruit varies in colour, shape and size, from green to yellow skins and from round to pear-shaped about 1–5 ins (2–12 cm) long. The dense, granular flesh, full of little seeds, has a strong, aromatic flavour, unique to the Guava – probably due to the presence of eugenol, an essential oil, also found in cloves. The flesh varies in colour from white to cream to pink. Guavas are used widely in the Caribbean for jams, jellies, pastes, drinks and desserts. Guava cheese, a heavy, paste-like sweet, covered in sugar and cut into squares is a great favourite. The aroma of Guavas cooking is not easily forgotten. Having medicinal qualities, the leaves and buds have been used for various stomach ailments.

Guava (*Psidium guajava*)

Syzygium aromaticum
Clove Tree

The Clove Tree came from Madagascar and is now found on most of the islands. It is grown commercially in Grenada, the 'Spice Island', where the nutmeg, cinnamon and vanilla are also grown. The tree grows to a height of 40 ft (12 m). The aromatic, leathery, green leaves appear reddish when young. Clusters of small, yellow, tubular flowers with red bases appear at the end of the branches. The flower buds are picked before they open and the commercial clove, as we know it, is the receptacle of that immature flower. It is then sun-dried, turning dark brown and woody, with a sweet, aromatic odour. Oil of cloves is used widely for toothache.

Syzygium cumini
Jambolan, Java Apple, Java Plum, Black Plum

Native to the East Indies, the Jambolan is found on some of the Caribbean islands. It is a medium-sized tree with oblong, glossy green leaves. The white flowers are followed by the dark reddish-purple fruits about 1 in (2.5 cm) long which are borne at the ends of the branches. When ripe, they resemble bunches of grapes. The flesh may be white or purple, depending on the variety. However, both have an acid flavour, although the white tends to be a bit sweeter. The Jambolan can be eaten fresh, but is usually used in jams, jellies and often in juices. The tree usually bears an abundance of fruit, so it should be planted away from the house.

Jambolan (*Syzygium cumini*)

Syzygium currantii
Lipote

The Lipote comes from the Philippines and makes a smallish tree growing to 20 ft (6 m) high. The oval leaves are about 6 ins (15 cm) long and have a deep wine colour when young, becoming medium green when mature. They make a beautiful show. The greyish bark of the trunk and the older branches resemble those of the common guava. The small fruits, about 1 in (2.5 cm) in diameter, are dark red when ripe. They are borne in short-stemmed clusters on the mature twigs. The pulp of the fruit is mildly acid and has a very attractive flavour. However, it is somewhat dry for eating fresh. The fruit is very high in pectin content and makes good jelly.

Lipote (*Syzygium currantii*)

Syzygium jambos
Rose Apple, Malay Apple

The Rose Apple comes from Malay and the East Indian islands. It was introduced to Jamaica in the late eighteenth century, where it was used as a shade tree for the coffee and cocoa plantations. It is a tall, striking tree with a dense top and drooping, spreading branches. We found some very tall ones in the mountains of St Vincent. The new leaves are pinkish, becoming dark green, 5–8 ins (12–20 cm) long and slender with maturity. The showy white flowers, 2–3 ins (5–8 cm) across, have a small tuft of stamens, making up the better part of the flower. The ripe fruit has a distinct rose-scented aroma and is pear-shaped, about 3 ins (5 cm) in diameter with a waxy, ivory-white skin tinged with pink. The white flesh is crisp, slightly dry, and rather insipid but with a distinct flavour of rose-petals. It surrounds a brown seed. Often used in jams and jellies, the fruit is also eaten raw but many people are put off by its rose-like flavour.

Rose Apple (*Syzygium jambos*)

Syzygium malaccense
Malay Apple, Pomerac, Water Apple

The Malay Apple comes from the large genus of *Syzgium*, but is still referred to as *Eugenia* by many of the Botanical Gardens around the world. Native to Malay, the tree was introduced to the Caribbean in the late eighteenth century by Captain Bligh. Often grown as an ornamental for the foliage as well as the flowers and fruit, this small tree has large glossy leaves from 7–12 ins (18–30 cm) long. Small, deep pink flowers, like little shaving brushes, appear on the trunk and larger branches. The Malay apple is not in the shape of an apple, as the name suggests, but more like a pear. The fruits are 2–3 ins (5–8 cm) in diameter with a thin, bright pink skin. The flesh is crisp, white and slightly sweet with little flavour. Malay Apples are eaten raw or cooked and used to make jams and jellies. It is a close relative of the Rose Apple and widely planted in the Caribbean.

Malay Apple (*Syzygium malaccense*)

Pimenta racemosa
Bay Rum Tree

The Bay Rum Tree is native to the West Indies. This large tree grows to about 40 ft (12 m) high and has peeling bark. Its dense, dark green crown is made up of small, stiff, leathery leaves which are more rounded than those of the Allspice (*Pimenta dioica*), its close relative. The small, white flowers appear in branched clusters followed by the brown, berry-like fruits containing a few seeds. The Bay Rum is grown commercially in the US Virgin Islands and Jamaica for the essential oils that are obtained from the leaves and small branches. Bay oil is used in cosmetics, hair products and medicines. The leaves are used widely in cooking.

Bay Rum Tree (*Pimenta racemosa*)

Psidium cattleianum
Strawberry Guava, Cattley Guava, Cherry Guava

The Strawberry Guava comes from Brazil and has not been in the Caribbean as long as the Guava. This small tree will sometimes grow to 25 ft (7.5 m) and makes a very pretty ornamental for the garden. The trunk has a scaly, grey-brown bark. Large clusters of glossy, thick, leathery, dark green leaves cover the branches. The white flowers are 1 in (2.5 cm) wide and are followed by the round, purplish-red fruits, also about 1 in (2.5 cm) in diameter. Thin skin surrounds the soft, whitish flesh which contains numerous seeds. The flavour is guava-like, sweet with a hint of strawberry, hence the name. The strawberry guava makes very good jelly – in some of the old cookery books the recipes call for a mixture of large guavas and strawberry guavas for good flavour.

Strawberry Guava (*Psidium cattleianum*)

Averrhoa bilimbi
Bilimbi, Blimbee

The Bilimbi, which originally comes from tropical Asia, reached the Caribbean at the end of the eighteenth century. It is found in many gardens throughout the region and there are several in the Botanical Gardens in St Vincent. The tree grows to about 30 ft (9 m) with upright branches. It can be easily distinguished from the Carambola as the leaves are much larger. Small, dark red flowers appear directly on the trunk and larger branches. These are followed by the fruits which are usually bunched together on the trunk and branches. These fruits are about 4 ins (10 cm) long, resembling an unridged pickle, and have a delicate, thin skin. Starting out green, the Bilimbi turns pale yellow when ripe. The extremely acid flesh is crisp and very juicy with a few seeds. Not often eaten raw, it is used as a relish with fish, to make jellies and is often preserved in a sugary syrup to make 'Bilimbi sauce'.

Bilimbi (*Averrhoa bilimbi*)

Averrhoa carambola
Carambola, Star Fruit, Cornichon

The Carambola originated in China, where it is grown both as an ornamental tree and for its fruit. The Portuguese introduced it to Brazil and then took it to the Caribbean. The spreading tree will normally grow to about 30 ft (9 m), although we have seen one that was well over 50 ft (15 m) in the 'wet lands' of Antigua. The light green leaves are unusual in having the capability of closing at night and opening again in the morning. They will also close in a high wind. The small, pinkish flowers have a pleasant fragrance. These are followed by the unusual, bright yellow, waxy fruits, which become an orangey-brown when ripe. They are about 4 ins (10 cm) long with five distinct ridges running from top to bottom. When cut in

slices, the fruit resembles a star, hence the name Star Fruit. The crisp, juicy, yellow flesh has a lemony-apple flavour. If eating them raw, be sure to pick a sweet one as the fruit can be very tart. They are used to make jellies and desserts, are served with fish or tossed in salads. The Carambola is difficult to produce commercially as it must ripen on the tree and spoils very quickly once picked. The fruit in the Far East tends to be much bigger than those growing in the Caribbean. There are several Carambola trees in the Botanical Gardens in St Vincent and they can also be seen in many backyard gardens throughout the Caribbean.

Carambola (*Averrhoa carambola*)

Cocos nucifera
Coconut

Probably one of the oldest trees around, the Coconut is found in all the tropical parts of the world. We usually associate Coconut trees with white beaches. However, they grow very well on the sides of mountains, as seen in Dominica, St Lucia, St Vincent and most of the mountainous islands. The tree has been important to the West Indies for hundreds of years, for its fruits, copra and wood. The trunk of the Coconut can grow up to 100 ft (30 m) tall. At the top it carries its magnificent leaves which can reach up to 20 ft (6 m) in length. As these fronds fall off, they leave a scar on the trunk surrounded by brown fibres, although most will stay attached to the tree for up to two years. It is here that the small bunches of flowers are to be found, followed by the fruits. The coconuts, which are not strictly nuts, form in greenish-yellow clusters. When the outer skin and husk are removed, the hard 'nut' is revealed. Depending on how ripe the fruit is, the 'nut' will contain either coconut water in the green fruit, coconut jelly in the greenish-yellow fruit or hard, white flesh in the very ripe yellowish-brown fruit. In the markets you might be asked if you want a 'waternut' or a 'coconut'. Throughout time the Coconut has provided man with the material to thatch roofs, make floor matting, fill mattresses and, last but not least, the oil for cooking and for filling lamps.

Coconut (*Cocos nucifera*)

Cocoloba uvifera
Sea Grape, Seaside Grape, Grape

The Sea Grape has been in the West Indies for hundreds of years. It can be seen on any seashore on most of the islands growing as a sprawling shrub. When grown inland the Sea Grape will grow upright to about 25 ft (7.5 m) high. The thick, leathery, round, red-veined leaves can be 8 ins (20 cm) across, and will stand a lot of wind. Some bushes produce only male flowers, while others produce the female flowers, the latter being the fruit bearer. The clusters of fruits hang just like bunches of small green grapes. When ripe, they have a purplish tinge. Although rather sour, they are a great favourite with children. The Sea Grape is used fairly widely for jam and jelly making. The red sap used to be used for tanning and dyeing.

Sea Grape (*Cocoloba uvifera*)

Punica granatum
Pomegranate

The Pomegranate, which comes from Africa and Asia, is one of the oldest recorded fruits. The 'forbidden apple' in the Garden of Eden is thought to have been the Pomegranate. The tree is small and shrubby. Often grown as an ornamental, it will usually only reach about 20 ft (6 m) high. The young leaves are red, turning green with maturity. The beautiful bell-shaped, red flowers appear on the branches, singly or in clusters of two or three. Some horticultural varieties have double flowers. The apple-sized fruits have a thick, leathery, shiny skin which is greenish-yellow with patches of red, becoming orangey-red when ripe. Inside the thick rind is a mass of white seeds in a dark red pulp. A very messy fruit to try and eat, it is also quite tart, although there are now some varieties that are almost seedless and much sweeter. Grenadine is made from the juice of the fruit and the rind is used in tanning and dyeing. It has been reported that the rind of the Pomegranate has anti-bacterial properties. The tree can be found on most of the islands, usually growing in small gardens.

Pomegranate (*Punica granatum*)

Zizyphus mauritania
Indian Jujube, Dunks

There are two species of *Zizyphus* cultivated in the Orient: *Z. jujuba* is the Chinese variety and *Z. mauritiana* is the Indian version. Now grown throughout the tropics, the spiny Jujube Tree grows to about 25 ft (7.5 m) high. The glossy, dark green leaves are 2–3 ins (5–8 cm) long with downy undersides. The small, greenish white flowers are borne on small branches and, occasionally, directly on the trunk. The oblong or roundish fruits vary in size from $\frac{1}{2}$–2 ins (1–5 cm) long, with a yellowish-brown skin containing white, sweet, slightly acidic flesh which encloses a hard two-part stone. Easily pruned, the spiny tree is often planted as a hedge. The fruits are used to make jams and jellies and the fresh fruit are a favourite with children.

Indian Jujube (*Zizyphus mauritania*)

Chrysobalanus icaco
Cocoplum, Icaco, Fat Pork

The Cocoplum comes from Central America and grows throughout the Caribbean. It is a small, shrubby tree reaching about 30 ft (9 m) in height, with dense, dark green foliage and is often planted as an ornamental. The thick glossy, ovate leaves are about 2 ins (5 cm) long. The small, white flowers are followed by the fruit. There are several species of *Chrysobalanus*, each one with a fruit of a slightly different colour. However, the Icaco or Cocoplum, has fruit resembling a large plum – slightly rose-scented, 1–2 ins (2–5 cm) long with a creamy white thin skin which becomes tinged with pink on ripening. The white, slightly cottony flesh sticks firmly to the large seed which has little taste. In Cuba the fruit is made into a sweet preserve.

Cocoplum (*Chrysobalanus icaco*)

Eriobotrya japonica
Loquat, Japanese Medlar

The Loquat originated in China and Japan, where it is one of the most important fruits. A member of the *Rosaceae* family, it is now widely grown in the tropics. The well-shaped tree grows to 25 ft (7.5 m) and has low, spreading branches. It is becoming a great favourite with landscapers and can often be found growing in parks and hotel grounds as an ornamental. The fuzzy, light green leaves become dark and leathery and grow up to 10 ins (25 cm) long. Clusters of creamy white flowers appear at the ends of the branches followed by large, loose clusters of fruit. The fruits are small, furry, pale yellow to orange, rather like small apricots. However, unlike the apricot, the Loquat may have up to five seeds. The fruits are used in jams and jellies and can be eaten directly from the tree, but tend to be rather tart.

Loquat (*Eriobotrya japonica*)

Coffea arabica
Coffee

Coffee is a native of Ethiopia and was being used by the Arabs in the fifteenth century. In the early eighteenth century, coffee drinking became very fashionable in Europe. Requiring tropical land to grow coffee, the French introduced a few small trees to the Caribbean, where they flourished. However, the Haitian revolution, which occurred during the early part of the eighteenth century, persuaded the French farmers to find alternative land. This was the beginning of the famous Jamaican coffee. By the end of the nineteenth century, coffee was Puerto Rico's main export.

It is now grown on many of the islands with Jamaican 'Blue Mountain' Coffee probably being the best known. Coffee grown at higher altitudes is usually of superior quality. That grown in the lowlands needs shade and is often seen growing in conjunction with avocados and bananas. The Coffee Tree grows to about 15 ft (4.5 m) but is usually kept shorter to facilitate harvesting. It is a bushy tree with short-stalked, shiny, dark green leaves and clusters of short-lived, small white flowers which have a jasmine-like fragrance. Coffee berries start out green, turning dark red with maturity. The coffee beans are handpicked and sun-dried. They can then be stored in this form until they are threshed and packed for export. Coffee is used throughout the world as a drink, as a flavouring for many cakes and desserts and it is also used in Jamaica's famous liqueur, Tia Maria.

Coffee (*Coffea arabica*)

Aegle marmelos
Bael Fruit

The Bael Fruit is native to India, where it is considered sacred in many parts of the country. Often called the Indian Quince, it is not, however, related to the true quince. The Bael is not often seen in the Caribbean, however it can be found in some botanical gardens and some of the older gardens. It is a small tree with thin, spiny branches planted more as an oddity than for its fruit. Small, white flowers are followed by the round fruits, which look a bit like dirty oranges, having a yellowish grey, hard skin containing sweet, orange, slightly pulpy flesh with many seeds. Bael fruit is not worth eating fresh, but is used to make drinks and jellies.

Bael Fruit (*Aegle marmelos*)

Casimiroa edulis
White Sapote

The White Sapote comes from the highlands of Central America and is not very well known outside its native country, although it is occasionally found in some of the Caribbean islands. This well-formed, open-growing tree of medium height has glossy, green leaves. The small, greenish-white flowers are followed by the fruits, which are the size of a small apple. These green fruits have a whitish pulp, while the yellow variety has a thin skin encasing a softish, yellow, custard-like pulp with between two and five seeds. The creamy flesh has a peculiar flavour, being sweet and bitter, which sometimes leaves a bitter aftertaste. The fruit is usually eaten raw as it does not stand up to cooking very well, but it can be made into a refreshing drink or ice cream. The White Sapote is reputed to contain soporific substances, which suggests that care should be taken when eating this fruit. The seeds were used medicinally by the Aztecs.

White Sapote (*Casimiroa edulis*)

Citrus aurantifolia
Lime

The Lime comes from South-East Asia and found its way to Europe from where Columbus was responsible for introducing it to the Caribbean. The much smaller Mexican or Key Lime is the variety more familiar in Florida and The Bahamas. This small shrubby tree grows to about 20 ft (6 m) and is irregular in growth form. The branches are thorny, bearing stiff, oval leaves 2–3 ins (5–8 cm) long. The self-pollinating, sweet-smelling, small, white

flowers have yellow stamens. The fruits vary in shape and size depending on the variety. The large, green West Indian Lime resembles a roundish lemon in shape and size. The flesh is very juicy and sweeter than the smaller Mexican Lime. Grown throughout the Caribbean, the Lime can be seen in most backyards. Lime juice, with its high ascorbic acid (vitamin C) level, became part of the British navy's diet to try and help combat scurvy, thus giving rise to the nickname 'Limey'. Some islands process large quantities of limes for export, Dominica being one of them. Lime oil is extracted from the rind and the lime is the main source of the citric acid used in the dyeing industry. It also has a wide range of medicinal uses.

Lime (*Citrus aurantifolia*)

Citrus aurantium
Sour Orange, Marmalade Orange, Seville

Originally from tropical Asia, the Spanish spread the Sour Orange through Europe and Columbus brought it to the West Indies. Apart from making marmalade, the Sour Orange has virtually no uses outside the Caribbean. However, in our region they have many uses in the islands from marinating fish and flavouring conch salad to making juice and flavouring drinks. The tree is medium-sized and well shaped with dense foliage and is often grown as an ornamental. The branches have long, spiky thorns and bright green leaves turning a glossy dark green with maturity. The small, white, fragrant

flowers have yellow stamens. It is quite common to see a Sour Orange Tree with flowers, green and ripe, orange fruit all at the same time. The ripe fruits are roundish, 3–4 ins (8–10 cm) in diameter with a rough skin resembling a sweet orange. The juicy pulp is extremely acid and has an abundance of seeds. The Sour Orange is often mistaken for the Bitter Sweet Orange which turns a much darker colour when ripe and is not quite as acidic. Medicinally, the juice of the Sour Orange is mixed together with Cerasse (*Mormordica charantia*) and boiled to make a hot tea, said to bring relief to flu and fevers. The rind of the Sour Orange is often candied. *Citrus aurantium curassuviensis* is an essential ingredient of the liqueur, Curacao. The Sour Orange Tree is used as rootstock for growing citrus in low moist areas.

Sour Orange (*Citrus aurantium*)

Citrus limon
Lemon

Like other members of the *Citrus* genus, the lemon probably came from tropical Asia. Columbus introduced it to Haiti in the late fifteenth century. Although not as popular as the Lime in the Caribbean, the Lemon can be found growing in many gardens in the West Indies. The tree is small with irregular growth and small, pale green leaves about 4 ins (10 cm) long. The small, white flowers are followed by the fruit which, when ripe, are generally oval, 3–4 ins (8–10 cm) long with a slight point at the end. The thick, slightly oily skin is lemon yellow in colour when ripe. The flesh is very juicy and acid with a distinct flavour. In the Caribbean, the Lime far outweighs the Lemon for flavouring drinks and its uses in cooking, but the Lemon can still hold its own in the kitchen.

Citrus maxima
Ugli, Ugli Fruit

The Ugli Fruit Tree was discovered in Jamaica in the early twentieth century and was probably the result of an accidental cross between an orange and a grapefruit. It is now found in many of the islands being grown in gardens for its fruit. The tree grows to much the same form as a grapefruit but not quite so tall. The fruit, resembling a grapefruit, has a loose-fitting, slightly wrinkled skin, varying in colour from light green to deep orange. The size varies from that of a large orange to an enormous grapefruit. The Ugli, regardless of its name and appearance, is a delightful fruit. The flesh is golden in colour, very juicy, with an acid sweet flavour, not as sweet as an orange and not as bitter as a grapefruit. It is very easy to peel and almost free of seeds. Jamaica is still exporting the Ugli on a small scale.

Citrus maxima grandis
Shaddock, Pummelo

The Shaddock, which originally comes from the South Pacific, was brought to the Caribbean by Captain Shaddock, who named this, the largest of all the citrus fruits. The tree grows in form much as the grapefruit – it is the fruits which are different. They can weigh up to 12 lbs (6 kg) with a very thick rind, which makes up the major part of the fruit. The rather coarse flesh resembles the grapefruit but the flavour is inferior. The Shaddock grows on many of the islands – there are some very good examples to be seen in Antigua.

Citrus mitis
Calamondin, Calamansi, Kalamondin

The Calamondin comes from the Philippines and is thought to be a hybrid of a tangerine and a kumquat. The tree is small but well formed, growing to about 20 ft (6 m). The leaves tend to be smaller than most citrus trees, but the white flowers are much the same as an orange. Small, round, orange-like fruit cover the tree and, whether it is grown for its fruit or not, it makes a very attractive ornamental. The very acid fruit is used mostly to make marmalade, preserves and for flavouring drinks. The juice can be used in the same way as lime juice and is very good squeezed over fruit.

Calamondin (*Citrus mitis*)

Citrus nobilis
Tangerine

The Tangerine is a small, spreading tree with thin branches and small, narrow, glossy, dark green leaves. Small, white, fragrant flowers are followed by the fruits which are usually 2–3 ins (5–8 cm) in diameter. Depending on the variety, the fruit can be greenish orange or bright orange when ripe. The skin becomes very loose, encasing the sweet, juicy, acidic flesh which readily divides into segments, making it very easy to eat out of hand.

Tangerine (*Citrus nobilis*)

Citrus paradisi
Grapefruit

Some experts say the Grapefruit originated in the West Indies, others will say
it is a cross between the Shaddock, which was brought to the West Indies by
Captain Shaddock, and the Pommelo. However, by the middle of the
nineteenth century, the Jamaicans were calling a fruit smaller than the
Shaddock and larger than the Pommelo, 'Grapefruit'. The Grapefruit Tree
is well formed, growing much taller than other members of the *Citrus*
genus, with a rounded crown. The stiff, dark green, glossy leaves are 5–6 ins
(13–15 cm) long. The white, scented flowers of the Grapefruit are much
larger than its cousins. The fruits vary greatly in size, shape and colour, but
are usually roundish with a greenish-lemon coloured thick skin. The flesh

can be white, reddish or pink, sweet and acidic with a high level of vitamin C, and it is now a breakfast favourite throughout the world. The Grapefruit Tree is found on most of the islands growing in many gardens. It used to be grown extensively in Puerto Rico for export to North America until large grapefruit groves sprung up in America.

Grapefruit (*Citrus paradisi*)

Citrus sinensis
Orange, Sweet Orange

Originally from tropical Asia, the Orange was brought to the Caribbean by the Spanish. Seen in most gardens throughout the islands, the Orange is a medium-sized tree with irregular growth. The first orange trees were grown from seed but today most varieties are almost always grafted, usually using the rootstock of the Sour Orange. Small white, fragrant flowers are followed by the fruit, which usually take nine months to ripen. Oranges vary widely in shape, depending on the variety. The Navel Orange is one of the more popular varieties because of its size, juice and sweet flesh. It is high in vitamin C and used all over the world for the 'eye opener' breakfast juice. Orange peel is used in the making of the liqueur, Cointreau.

Orange (*Citrus sinensis*)

Fortunella margarita
Kumquat

Many commercial growers still refer to the Kumquat as a *Citrus*, although many botanists disagree. It was renamed *Fortunella* after the explorer, Robert Fortune, who decided it was not a *Citrus*, although it does make very good marmalade. The Kumquat is a native of China and Japan. It is now grown extensively in Florida and has made its way down through the Caribbean islands. The Kumquat is grown more as an ornamental, and may be seen in the more specialised gardens. Often grown in tubs, it will reach about 6 ft (1.8 m). However, grown in open ground it will reach 15 ft (4.5 m). The leaves are leathery, dark green and citrus-like. The clusters of small, white flowers have an orange-blossom aroma. The fruit is like a small orange, about 1 in (2.5 cm) in diameter, with a thin, sweet skin that can be eaten along with the flesh. Since the crop of plum-sized, orange fruits can be heavy, care should be taken to protect the tree from wind. Kumquats are used as a garnish. When very ripe, they are eaten whole although they can be very acidic. They make very good marmalade and preserves.

Kumquat (*Fortunella margarita*)

Triphasia trifolia
Limeberry

The Limeberry is probably native to southern Asia and is occasionally found in the Caribbean. A small, shrubby tree growing to about 15 ft (4.5 m) high, it is covered in very spiky thorns and leathery, dark green leaves, about 2 ins (5 cm) long. It is widely used as a hedge plant. Small, white, fragrant flowers form singly in the leaf axils. These are followed by the small, dark red berries which have a large seed in the middle covered with a small amount of syrupy pulp. The fruit is usually used to make jams and preserves.

Limeberry (*Triphasia trifolia*)

Blighia sapida
Akee, Aki, Ackee

The Akee comes from Africa and was brought to the Caribbean by Captain Bligh in the eighteenth century, reaching Jamaica in 1778 where it is now the national tree. It is cultivated on many of the West Indian islands. The tree grows to about 40 ft (12 m) high with an open crown, stiff branches and oblong leaves 4–6 ins (10–15 cm) long. Small, greenish-white flowers are followed by the curious-looking fruit. At a distance, the Akee fruits resemble large red and yellow oblong plums. On closer inspection, you will probably find some have opened to reveal the three shiny black seeds, rather like crabs' eyes watching you! The yellow fruit takes on a red blush when ripe and when the rind splits, the three large, black seeds can be seen nestling in the creamy-coloured aril – it is this aril which is the edible part. When cooked, Akee resembles lumpy scrambled eggs, having a very delicate texture. It is especially excellent with salt fish. Care should be taken to pick Akee at exactly the right time, as if used before it splits open naturally, the aril is said to be poisonous. It is also supposed to be poisonous if it gets soft and old. The wood of the Akee Tree is used on many of the islands for carving.

Akee (*Blighia sapida*)

Euphorbia longana
Longan

The Longan, a close relative of the Lychee (*Litchi chinensis*) also came from China. It is grown as an ornamental as well as for its fruits and is an attractive tree growing to about 30 ft (9 m) high, having a well-rounded crown and glossy green leaves 3–6 ins (8–15 cm) long. Clusters of small, greenish-white flowers appear at the ends of the branches. Large clusters of fruit are produced. Each Longan is round, about 1 in (2.5 cm) in diameter, with a reddish-brown, pimply skin enclosing white flesh surrounding a round seed. It is held to be sweeter but not as juicy as the Lychee. The fruit is usually eaten fresh, although it is not nearly as good as the Lychee.

Litchi chinensis
Lychee, Litchi

The Lychee comes from Southern China, where it has been cultivated for more than 2 000 years. It is occasionally found in the Caribbean, usually in the higher elevations. There are some particularly good specimens in The Bahamas. A very elegant tree, the Lychee grows to about 40 ft (12 m) with a densely-covered, rounded crown. The pendulous branches are covered with glossy leaves, reddish when young, turning pale green with maturity. When flowering, the tree gives the appearance of having a haze around it as it is covered with clusters of small greenish-white flowers at the ends of the branches. The clusters of fruits look like hanging bunches of strawberries and can have many as 20 on each stem. Each round fruit is 1–2 ins (2.5–5 cm) in diameter with a tough, pimply, almost brittle skin, either red or yellow in colour. Inside, the fleshy, white, gelatinous pulp surrounds a large, glossy, dark brown seed. The Lychee Tree does not bear fruit every year. If you like canned Lychees, the fresh Lychee will be a joy.

Lychee (*Litchi chinensis*)

Melicocca bijuga

Mamoncillo, Spanish Lime, Genip, Jamaica Plum, Limoncillo

The Spanish Lime or Genip is native to the Caribbean and Central America. A slow-growing, well-formed, shapely tree, it grows to about 60 ft (18 m) and has a greyish bark and pale green leaves. The short clusters of small flowers are either male or female so it is necessary to have both to produce fruit. Clusters of round, green fruit, each about 1 in (2.5 cm) in diameter, hang from the ends of the smaller branches. A smooth, thick, green skin contains the juicy, almost translucent, yellowish-pink flesh, surrounding a large round seed. The best way to eat a Genip, is to peel off the top of the thick skin and squeeze the fruit into your mouth – worth the effort, although they can sometimes be as sour as a lime (from where it gets the name Spanish Lime or Limoncillo). Towards the end of the summer, stems of grape-like bunches of Genips can be seen for sale along the roadsides – unfortunately you can see the shells of the Genips scattered all around as well! On some islands the fruit is processed to make juice.

Spanish Lime (*Melicocca bijuga*)

Chrysophyllum cainito
Star Apple, Star Plum, Cainite, Mexican Custard Apple

The Star Apple comes from the same family as the Sapodilla, and has been in the West Indies for hundreds of years. Found in most of the Caribbean islands, it is used primarily as a shade tree due to its dense foliage. An attractive garden tree, it will grow to about 50 ft (15 m) with leaves that are dark green on the upper side and a silvery-copper colour on the under side. When the wind blows these leaves produce a shimmering effect. Small, white flowers are followed by the apple-sized, purple or greenish-white skinned fruits. When sliced in half, the star shape is revealed, which results from the way the small, black seeds are set in a translucent jelly amongst the purplish flesh. The fruit needs to be ripened on the tree, as immature fruits have a gummy taste. This makes it difficult to export. The purple Star Apples tend to have more flavour, while the green ones are a little sweeter. Used mainly in fruit salads, the Star Apple can also be eaten on its own.

Star Apple (*Chrysophyllum cainito*)

Manilkara zapotilla
Sapodilla, Dilly, Naseberry, Sapotille

A native of the West Indies, Mexico and Central America, the Sapodilla is one of the more elegant fruit trees in the Caribbean. Slow-growing, the well-shaped tree will eventually reach 50 ft (15 m) high with spreading branches and dense foliage. The tough, shiny green leaves are oblong and 5 ins (13 cm) long. The Sapodilla produces small, greenish-white flowers several times a year. The orange-sized fruit has a pale brown, roughish, mat skin and is about 4 ins (10 cm) in diameter when ripe. The flesh, which ranges from creamy-white to dark brown, has a granular consistency, rather like cooked pears, and contains shiny black seeds. The fruit, which is very sweet, is considered slightly sickly by many, but it is usually very popular with children. Unripe fruits contain tannin and taste very bitter. The fruits are used in jams, ice creams and fruit salads. The bark of the Sapodilla produces a latex called 'chicle', an ingredient of chewing-gum. However, great care should be taken to only tap these trees once every eight years as many trees have died from being tapped too often.

Sapodilla (*Manilkara zapotilla*)

Pouteria campechiana
Canistel, Yellow Sapote, Egg Fruit

Native to tropical America, the Canistel is found on most of the Caribbean islands and it is especially popular in Cuba. The well-formed tree grows to about 20 ft (6 m) with bright green, oblong leaves about 6 ins (15 cm) long. Clusters of three or four small flowers appear on the young branches. The glossy skinned, bright orange fruit can be roundish, egg-shaped or plump with pointed ends and is usually 4–6 ins (10–15 cm) long. The thin skin is bitter, while the very sweet, sometimes musky flesh has the cloying consistency of cooked egg-yolk which some people find slightly sickly. The fruit usually contains two or three shiny, dark brown seeds. Generally picked before it ripens, the Egg Fruit can be eaten raw. However, many prefer it made into desserts, due to its very rich, sweet content.

Canistel (*Pouteria campechiana*)

Pouteria sapota
Sapote, Mamey Sapote, Mammee-Sapota, Zapotilla

The Sapote is indigenous to Central America and is a great favourite throughout the Caribbean. This large spreading tree can reach up to 60 ft (18 m) high and has tough, pointed leaves which are dark green on the upper side and greyish green on the underside. Small, insignificant flowers appear in profusion along the young branches followed by the fruit which appears directly on the branches. The brown, rough skinned fruit, ranges from 3–8 ins (8–20 cm) long with a pointed end. It is very hard to tell when the fruit is ripe, as it doesn't change colour. It is usually picked when still hard to avoid the damage which might occur from falling to the ground. Inside the toughish skin, the flesh is reddish-orange, slightly granular, sweet and very rich, with one or two glossy brown seeds. The richness of the fruit can be helped with a little lime juice. The fruit does not cook well as stewed fruit but will make very good jam, ice cream and sherbets.

Sapote (*Pouteria sapota*)

Theobroma cacao
Cocoa, Chocolate Tree

Cocoa originally came from the Amazon Basin in South America, where the Aztecs were growing it. The Spanish took the fascinating bitter chocolate paste back to Europe in the sixteenth century. Discovering its popularity and needing somewhere to grow Cocoa, they introduced it to the Caribbean where large plantations quickly sprang up. Of the three main varieties of Cocoa, the Trinitanio is the one most commonly found in the West Indies. The Cocoa prefers shady conditions, and is often found growing in conjunction with Coconuts and Bananas. A slow-growing tree, the Cocoa will grow to about 35 ft (10.5 m), but is usually kept to 15 ft (4.5 m) to make harvesting easier. The young, oblong, pendulous leaves are red, about 12 ins (30 cm) long, turning green and leathery with maturity. Small, yellow flowers appear in clusters directly on the trunk or on the larger branches. The tree will start producing fruit at about four years, but won't come into full production for seven to eight years. The oblong Cocoa pods are about 8–10 ins (20–25 cm) long, reddish-yellow in colour, with a ribbed, pimply and rough skin. After picking, the pods are cut open and sun dried to remove the mucous from around the seeds. The beans are then roasted and ground into a chocolate paste. Cocoa is now used extensively throughout the world for drinks, desserts, chocolate and of course chocolate cake! Chocolate, as such, is not used much in the islands, but the little sticks of cocoa paste are used to make a hot cocoa drink heavily laden with sugar.

Cocoa (*Theobroma cacao*)

Index

Note: page numbers in italics refer to illustrations on separate pages from the text